Stuck
to the
Ice

by Kate Scott
Illustrated by Bill Ledger

OXFORD
UNIVERSITY PRESS

In this story ...

Jin

Jin can zoom up and up.
He can go as high as a rocket.

Cam

Mr Trainer
(teacher)

Slink

Mr Trainer and the class were outside next to the pond.

"Mrs Molten has made a new tool," Mr Trainer said. "You will like this!"

Mr Trainer took out a long, blue stick. He hit a button and a jet of ice shot out. He used the stick to make the pond freeze.

It was time for the heroes to test their skills on the ice!

The class darted around on the ice. Even Slink had a go!
Jin kept falling down.
"Here, let me help you," said Cam.

"Can you make us a jump?" Cam asked.
"Yes," replied Mr Trainer. "Here goes ..."

Jin went whizzing down the ice jump.
It was like a steep valley.

An odd sound came out of the blue stick. Then
lots of ice blasted out of it!
"Oh dear," said Mr Trainer in dismay. "I think
it's broken!"

The ice froze the children's skates. They were stuck to the ice. Slink was stuck too.

"I'm freezing!" said Cam. "My feet are like ice cubes."

My whiskers are like icicles!

Then the stick went *CLUNK!* No more ice blasted out. "Phew!" said Mr Trainer, putting the stick down. "Now, how can I get you all off the ice?"

"I can fix this!" Jin said.
He flew out of his skates. Then he shot off to save Slink.

Jin lifted Cam off the ice. Then he went back to help the rest of the class.

The class gave a cheer.
"I may not be good at skating, but I'm good at rescuing!" said Jin.

Retell the story ...